Inspire Kindness

I was standing on my own, but no one cared.
I was tanned and skinny and raven-haired.
In a classroom full of kids,
I didn't look the way they did.

I was so uncomfortable and could just curl.
Although I'm not a super nervous kind of girl.
To be the new kid on the block
Had really come as quite a shock.

"My name is Lily," I said to everyone.
"I think school is very fun.
My favorite subject is reading.
And I like social studies, recess, and eating."

So I found my desk and settled down
But the boy who sat beside me wore a frown.
From the look upon his face,
I don't think he wanted me in this place.

I admit I found the classes very tough
For my English maybe wasn't good enough.
Many words were not the same.
I wish it could be as fun as a game.

Then, I realized I forgot my pencil and pen.
And the teacher said, "I won't say this again.
If you're hoping to succeed,
Be sure you have everything you need."

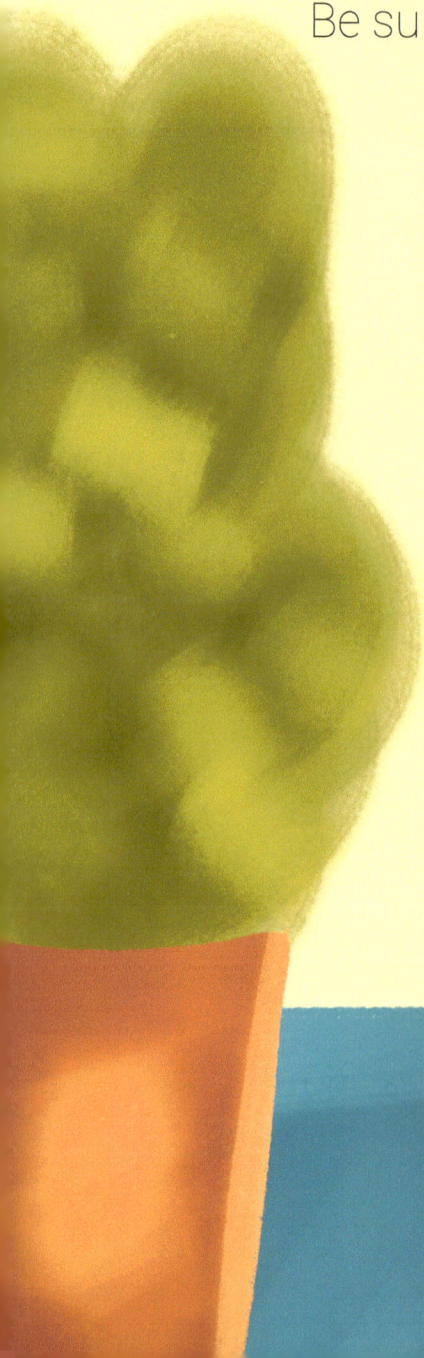

During lunch, the other kids were kind of rude
As I sat alone to eat my food.
And I didn't get my wish
For my favorite ethnic dish.

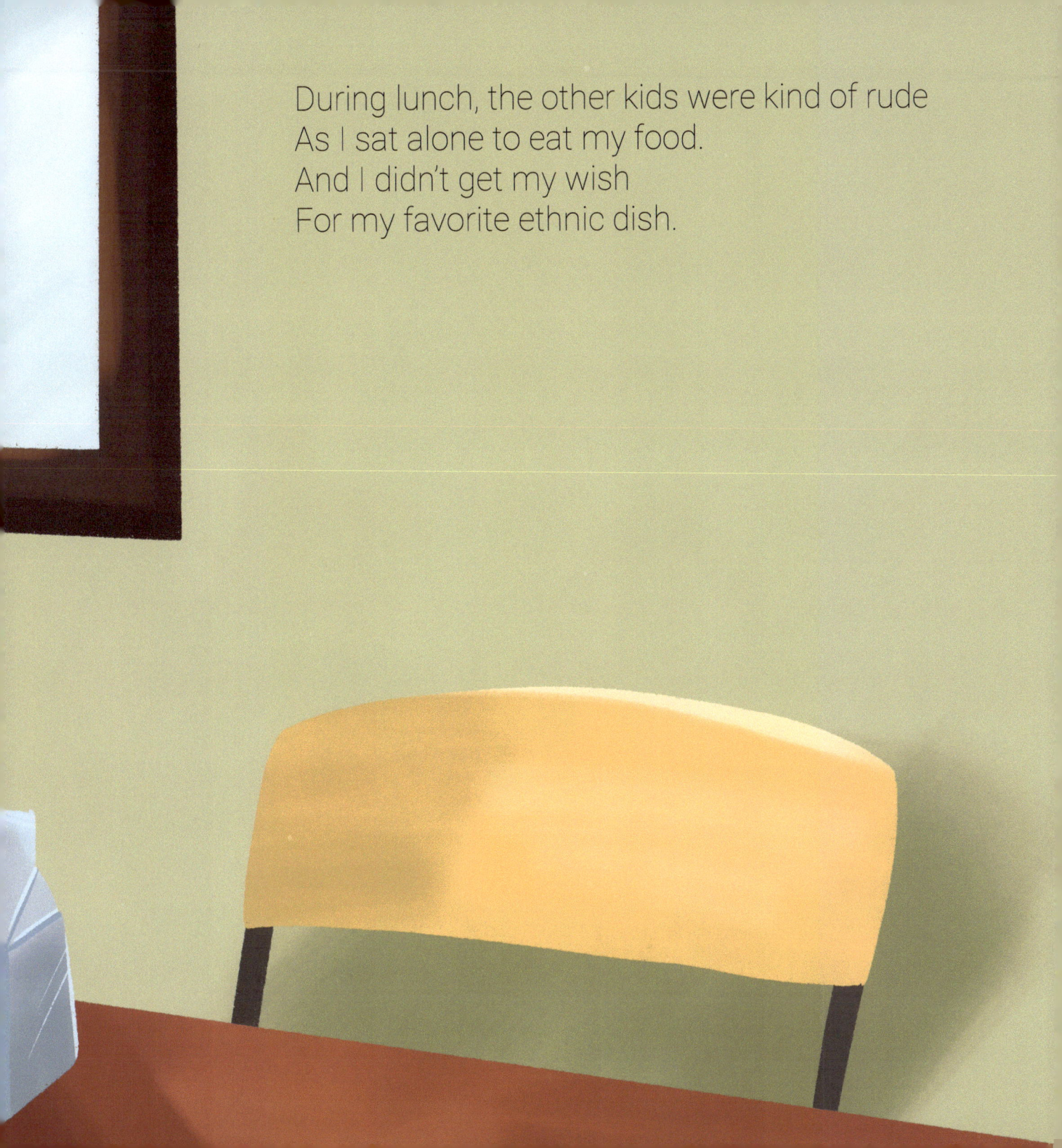

When they sent us out for recess, it was clear
That some students didn't think I should be here.
I would have liked to stay inside.
And my sadness couldn't be denied.

So, I sat and watched them playing with a ball
As they acted like I wasn't there at all.
And I wondered deep within
If I'd ever quite fit in.

I simply didn't want to be misunderstood.
And I promised I'd convince them if I could.
If only I could make one good friend...
One person - I wish the heavens would send.

KIDS!

Then just before they called us into class,
A student came to talk to me, at last.
What she said to me was, "Hi Lily!
Pleased to meet you, I'm Tilly."

Every word she said to me was a wonderful surprise.
All the doubt and fear vanished from my eyes.
I felt so happy I could shout
After feeling so very left out.

From that touch of kindness that she shared
Grew hope that can never be compared.
My heart soared and I felt so happy
All because someone cared, you see.

ACTS OF KINDNESS

1. Say thanks for no reason.
2. Leave a kind note in a library book you borrowed.
3. Make a friend laugh: Write a funny joke and leave it on someone's desk.
4. Smile at someone.
5. Be a study buddy or help a younger kid with home work.
6. After your meal, clear your own dishes. Then, clear your parent's dishes, too.
7. Let your sibling go first.
8. Leave some coins at the cash register for those in need.
9. Start a toy drive.
10. Leave a thank you note for your postman.
11. Give a compliment.
12. Make your mom's bed one morning.

13. Let someone go in front of you in line.
14. Ask someone to play or join in on the fun.
15. Help around the house with chores without being asked.
16. Bring in the mail for a neighbor.
17. Write a thank you card for a teacher or an educator in your life.
18. Volunteer your time for a local shelter.
19. Invite someone outside of your usual crowd to sit at your table at lunchtime.
20. Collect food and canned goods for a local food bank.
21. Be kind to a classmate you don't know.
22. Clean your room without being asked to.
23. Donate sports equipment and electronics you are no longer using.
24. Praise a friend who gets the answer right in class.

Make Someone SMILE Calendar

Let a sibling go first **1**	Say something nice to someone **2**
Hold the door for someone **6**	Volunteer **7**
Pick up trash **11**	Say thank you **12**
Make a care package **16**	Make someone's bed **17**
Donate your time to a shelter **21**	Make a gratitude jar **22**

Share **3**	Make kindness notes **4**	Play with someone new **5**
Make a handmade gift **8**	Say I love you **9**	Say hi to someone **10**
Say good job **13**	Give a compliment **14**	Say sorry if you do something wrong **15**
Offer a smile to a stranger **18**	Lend someone a hand **19**	Give away used toys and musical/sports equipment **20**
Write in a gratitude journal **23**	Tell someone how much you appreciate them **24**	Leave a kind note **25**

Dear Reader,

Thank you for reading my book. I hope you enjoyed "Inspire Kindness." I put a lot of thought and love into this book while creating it. This is my first book and it took me nearly ten years to publish it. I didn't know if or how, but I found a way. You know how the old saying goes, "Where there's a will, there's a way." I guess that happened to me with this book. I felt a calling in my heart to publish it as soon as my children were born. I know that the world is a beautiful place if we can just hold it in our hearts to inspire kindness. I would love to continue this series about emotions and feelings.

So please let me know what you liked and disliked. What kind of emotion would you like to see in my next book?

I'd love to hear from you. Please write to me at lilylopez.author@gmail.com

I would also greatly appreciate it if you could review my book. Your opinion matters a lot to me!

With love,
Lily

www.ingramcontent.com/pod-product-compliance
Lightning Source LLC
Chambersburg PA
CBHW042025090426
42811CB00016B/1738